contents

Rapping on the Window

CHRIS S. STEPHENS

ILLUSTRATED BY
SUZANNE CARPENTER

PONT *poetry*

First Impression – 2004

ISBN 1 84323 360 6

© Text: Chris S. Stephens
© Illustrations: Suzanne Carpenter

This book is published with the financial support of the
Welsh Books Council.

Printed in Wales at
Gomer Press, Llandysul, Ceredigion SA44 4JL

rap around wales

Rap around, rap around
Rap around Wales
Rap across the mountains
To the seashore and the vales.

Rap up and down Snowdon through the mists of grey
From Llandudno Junction to Carmarthen Bay.
Over the Preselis on the Drovers' way –
  Drovers' way! What did you say?
  You . . .

Rap around, rap around
Rap around Wales
Rap across the mountains
To the seashore and the vales.

Rap along the beach from Prestatyn to Rhyl
From Barry to Barmouth 'cos you can't keep still,
At Freshwater West you can drink your fill –
  Drink your fill! You can do it till,
  You . . .

Rap around, rap around
Rap around Wales
Rap across the mountains
To the seashore and the vales.

Rap into a castle where the Normans lurk
At Kidwelly and Beaumaris with your dagger and your dirk
Conwy and Caerphilly and the battlements at Chirk –
　　Chirk, Chirk! It's fun, not work,
　　When you . . .

　　　　Rap around, rap around
　　　　Rap around Wales
　　　　Rap across the mountains
　　　　To the seashore and the vales.

Rap around the islands; jump to the ground
Steep Holm, Flat Holm, Grassholm bound.
Are Bardsey, Caldey and Ramsey Sound?
　　Ramsey Sound! What have you found?
　　When you . . .

　　　　Rap around, rap around
　　　　Rap around Wales
　　　　Rap across the mountains
　　　　To the seashore and the vales.

　　　　What have you found?
　　　　It's a gift from me –
　　　　Wrapped up in Wales
　　　　Is the countryside that's free!

llandudno fishing rap

Let's go fishing at the end of the pier
Past Punch and Judy and the souvenir.
Tie some meat to a length of string
Drop it in the water, what'll it bring?

    Edible crab
    Seawater dab –
    Could be tasty nosh
    When it's dressed up fab!

Toss it in the bucket with the rest of the catch.
Who's going to win this fishing match?

    Fistful of blenny
    Not too many –
    Could be worth a lot
    Or less than ten a penny!

Toss it in the bucket with the rest of the catch.
Who's going to win this fishing match?

    Razor shell
    Mollusc as well –
    Could be the cause
    Of this awful smell!

Toss it in the bucket with the rest of the catch.
Who's going to win this fishing match?

>Crayfish tail
>No white whale –
>Could be sharper
>Than a rusty nail!

Toss it in the bucket with the rest of the catch.
Who's going to win this fishing match?

>Ragworms wriggle
>Both ends jiggle –
>Could be sea-spaghetti
>That makes Mum giggle!

Toss it in the bucket with the rest of the catch.
Who's going to win this fishing match?

>Starfish live
>Jiggle and jive –
>Could be fishy fingers
>So give me five!

Toss it in the bucket with the rest of the catch.
Who's going to win this fishing match?

Rusty can
What a scam –
Could chuck it back
For the next fisherman!

Toss it in the bucket with the rest of the catch.
Who's going to win this fishing match?

> Lizard in the sand
> Hold it in your hand –
> Could be a gecko
> From the Promised Land!

Toss it in the bucket with the rest of the catch.
Who's going to win this fishing match?

> Mermaid's purse
> Could be worse –
> Could be a notepad
> Of terrible verse!

Toss it in the bucket with the rest of the catch.
I know that I'm the winner of this fish-rap match!
Fish-rap match! Fish-rap catch!
I know that I'm the winner of the fish-rap match!

jemima's marching song

Get rapping on the windows, get tapping on the drums
Get your shawl and get your hat, before the French Invasion
                                                    comes.

       It's seventeen-ninety-seven
       They've sailed round the coast of Devon
       Now they've spied the Land of Heaven
       In the distance.
       They've seen a sign for Abergwaun
       And they think that they'll be fine
       But they've reckoned without mine
       And your resistance!

Black hat tall
Scarlet shawl
Pitchfork 'n'all
We're out to have a Ball . . .
       Every one a red-coat soldier
       We couldn't be much bolder
       Standing shoulder to shoulder
       On our road to victory . . .
       with . . .
       Jemima! Jemima!
       In her costume (Designer)
       No words can yet define 'er
       Courage and 'er glee.

There's a message from Lord Cawdor,
"You've to get your girls in order
And quick march towards the border
Where Pembroke County meets the sea."

As the cobbler hits the cobbles
She is just the one who nobbles
Every sea-sick frog who wobbles
Up the path to Fishguard Town,

Where we've got our own defences
To outwit those beastly Frenchies.
We will fight them on the beaches
And we'll fight them without breeches!
We don't need to dig out trenches
We're the craftiest Welsh wenches –
In the moonlight
We're the soldiers of King George! . . . so . . .

Get rapping on the windows, get tapping on the drums
Get your shawl and get your hat, before the French Invasion
comes.

Yes! Get rapping on the windows, get tapping on the drums
Get your shawl and get your hat, because Jemima's army
comes!

mari lwyd party

We are four young men, like you've never seen before,
The *Mari Lwyd* party who've reached your door
Rapping on the shutters, and stamping on the floor
With the . . .

> Old grey mare
> Glassy-eyed stare
> Skull that's bare
> Stroke it if you dare –
> But girls, beware
> Of the Mari Lwyd, Mari Lwyd
> Mari Lwyd mare.

Here we come a–wassailing upon this frosty night
Lighting up the darkness with a sheet of ghostly white
Round a horse of bells and ribbons and a *very* nasty bite
From the . . .

> Old grey mare
> Glassy-eyed stare
> Skull that's bare
> Stroke it if you dare –
> But girls, beware
> Of the Mari Lwyd, Mari Lwyd
> Mari Lwyd mare.

We're all wrapped up 'cos it's snappy out here,
We need to sup your ale and your strong brown beer.
Then we'll give you maids a taste of our New Year cheer
With the . . .

> Old grey mare
> Glassy-eyed stare
> Skull that's bare
> Stroke it if you dare –
> But girls, beware
> Of the Mari Lwyd, Mari Lwyd
> Mari Lwyd mare.

> SO THERE!

lanzarote funtime!

Leave Cardiff airport on an evening flight
Reach Arricife in the middle of the night
Wake up in the morning to the sunshine bright
In the . . .

> Lanzarote sunrise, some deep heat!
> Lanzarote sunset, your holiday treat!

Drive through the Lava and the Mountains Black
Catch yourself a camel, climb upon its back,
Following Diablo through the dusty desert track
To the . . .

> Lanzarote sunrise, some deep heat!
> Lanzarote sunset, your holiday treat!

Hit the Sunday market in old Teguise town
Buy yourself a fighting cloak or bright flamenco gown
Coat yourself with suncream and watch your skin go brown
Under . . .

> Lanzarote sunrise, some deep heat!
> Lanzarote sunset, your holiday treat!

17

Eating out in Tapas bars, and restaurants in craters,
Being serenaded by the handsome Spanish waiters
Chewin' baby squid and Canaries potaters
Grown in . . .

> Lanzarote sunrise, some deep heat!
> Lanzarote sunset, your holiday treat!

Speeding back to Cardiff with a suitcase full of sand,
A sombrero on your head and maracas in your hand
You'll be back to school on Monday – won't that just be
grand?
Forgettin' . . .

> Lanzarote sunrise, some deep heat!
> Lanzarote sunset, your holiday treat!

> Lanzarote suntime only lasts a week
> Lanzarote funtime, with César Manrique !

roundhead routers rap

For the children of Haverfordwest VC School

Colby Moor! Colby Moor!
An important Welsh battle in the English Civil War!

Colby Moor! Colby Moor!
Who was fighting who? Now are you sure?

Cavaliers, Roundheads, which is which?
Who was left bleeding in Colby ditch?

Royalists looting for harvest corn
Left Ha'fodwest on Friday morn.
Marched out bravely with hundreds of men
Couldn't believe it suddenly when . . .

Out jumped the Roundheads
Hiding in the field
With Laugharne's musketeers
Their Knot was Sealed.

They fell upon the Foot
And chased away the Horse
The Royalists were beaten
By a Parliamentary force.

Roundheads were winners
With a very high score
Marched proudly into Ha'rford
From Colby Moor.

Ransacked the garrison
And many others too,
Manorbier, Picton
And the castle of Carew!

Colby Moor! Colby Moor!
A battlefield close to your own front door!

Visit it now – imagine being alive
When the Cavaliers were routed in sixteen forty five!

sherwood supper rap

Merry Men of Sherwood, who can we see
Cooking up supper 'neath the greenwood tree?
Is it John Little, Allan Dale, Friar Tuck or such?
What's Marian made? Does Robin cook? – not Much!

    Venison pies,
    Brawny and wise,
    Opposite size
    Hey, you guys!

        It's big Little John
        Walking boots on,
        Soon be among –

Those Merry Men of Sherwood, whom we can see
Cooking up supper 'neath the greenwood tree.

    Minstrel sweet,
    Rhythm's off beat,
    Grilling wild boar's feet –
    Come on, let's greet

        Allan-a-Dale
        Lovesick and pale
        With a tuneful tale –

For those Merry Men of Sherwood, whom we can see
Cooking up supper 'neath the greenwood tree.

> Belching gabbit
> Casseroled rabbit
> In unclean habbit
> Just don't grabbit –
>> It's plump Friar Tuck
>> Taking one last look
>> At his stir-fry book –

With those Merry Men of Sherwood, whom we can see
Cooking up supper 'neath the greenwood tree.

> Sweet of face
> In Nottingham lace
> Rolling pastry case –
> Make some space
>> For Marian the Maid
>> With the table laid
>> And the compliments paid

To those Merry Cooks of Sherwood – but where's their
leader bold?
"Supper's on the table – it will soon be cold!"

Leader Robin
Hood
could
be hiding in the beech
wood
be stealing from the 'riche'
Lud
Savoury quiche
good
or Marian's summer
pud?

Served up in Sherwood, on the leafy forest floor
A feast of festive fayre from The Greenwood Four!

the ballad of Swansea Jack

Another day, another dollar
For the black Labrador with the silver collar.
Not a jack-tarred Swansea sailor he
But a maritime heritage celebrity.

    Born downtown in Padley Yard
    The meat was tough and the bones were hard
    But Swansea Jack and Master Bill
    Pawtrolled the docks with retrieving skill.

    He came to fame in '31
    Savin' a life that had just begun
    In a matter of weeks he'd saved another,
    The children's lifeguard, the kids' Big Brother.

    Before you could blink, or wag your tail
    His name was in *The Mirror* and the *Western Mail.*
    Soon *The Star* spread his fame abroad –
    With 'Bravest Dog of the Year' award.

    The Mayor of London rode into town
    With a trophy for Jack and an ermine gown.
    Life was OK in the canine saloon
    Breakfast at Crufts – a snooze 'til noon.

With 27 rescues notched up on his lead
The National Defence League all agreed
That Swansea Jack deserved a double –
Two bronze medals for his doggie-paddle trouble.

But his luck couldn't last. You've heard men say
That every dog will have his day.
Jack had his – and his name on a bullet –
Poisoned rat food in his gullet!

They couldn't save him – the Defence League tried –
But Swansea Jack lay down and died,
And there on the promenade near Swansea Bay
His tombstone remains to this very day.

No more days and no more dollars
For the black Labrador with the silver collars,
No more playing the rescue game
But his name lives on in the Kennel of Fame.

rugby rumba

Rugby: tug me,
tackle me if you dare
but don't try to convert me,
I've tried it and I swear
down at the National Stadium,
running with the ball,
with Shirley, Max and Bryn Terfel –
– we're the greatest stars of all . . .

Doing the   rugby club   rumba
Training Spring   Autumn and   Sumba
Marking our   opposite   numba
          across the . . . Millenni . . . um turf.

Fly half or   scrum half or   hookers
May not be   very good   lookers
We're every   one's fav'rite   ruckers
          down on the . . . Milleni . . . um earth.

Fancy dress   isn't for   Welsh lads
Scarlet shirts   gum shields and   shin pads
Designer boots   paid for by   proud dads
          for play on . . . Millenni . . . um turf.

Dancing round	opposing	wingers
Cheered on by	opera	singers
We are the	try-scoring	winners

success on . . . Millenni . . . um earth.

Wooden spoons	only bring	downers
Dreams of sweet	vict'ry a-	round us
Let's be the	next triple	crowners

show them what . . . Millenni . . . um's worth.

Jubilant	fans and sup-	porters
Hanging round	dressing room	quarters
Rugby wives	girlfriends and	daughters

in love with . . . Millenni . . . um turf.

WHEN THEY SEE US . . .

Doing the	rugby club	rumba
Training Spring	Autumn and	Sumba
Marking our	opposite	numba

across the . . . Millenni . . . um turf.

1 potato, 2 potato,
3 potato rap

I'm telling you now
If you haven't yet heard
There's more to a puffin
Than a stripy-beaked bird.
Puffins are potatoes
They're a county-wide brand
Grown at Angle and at Lamphey
And on Burton's sandy land.

There's *Premier* and *Rocket*,
These varieties taste good,
There's even *Lady Crystal* –
She's a very classy spud!
To call her just 'potato'
Would be nothing less than rude
There's no flies or eyes upon her
She's the princess of fine food.

When springtime turns to summer
And there's no more touch of frost
We'll be rolling back the plastic
We'll be pushing up the cost!
There'll be farmers digging 'Earlies'
No one wanting to be late
With their pickers and their graders
And their signs outside the gate.

There'll be lorry drivers hurrying
To markets through the night
Carrying potato sacks
All packed together tight –
On the road to England
With Welsh feathers in their cap
Putting Pembrokeshire potatoes
On the vegetable map!

Charles Dickens didn't sleep here!

What the Dickens did he say? What the Dickens did he write?
Where the Dickens did he wander in the middle of the night?

Down-town London! Up-town Paris!
Even spent a night in Castle Street in Beaumaris!

They served old-established cookery in 'Ye Olde Bull's Head'
But our *Uncommercial Traveller* missed his breakfasting in bed.
All day, every day for *All the Year Around*
He patrolled the beach at Moelfre and reported what he found.

The Royal Charter hit the waves and it hit the headlines too,
Our man Charlie on the scene – he knew just what to do . . .

He went to meet the vicar, talked of spirits from the past,
Souls returning from Australia who'd drowned before the mast.
He went to see the divers and the lifters of the gold
That was scattered on the seabed, when *The Charter* split her
hold.
He told her story in *The Shipwreck* to be read by you and me,
Of that fateful storm of fifty nine, off the coast of Anglesey.

What the Dickens did he say? What the Dickens did he write?
Where the Dickens did he wander in the middle of the night?

He was scribbling in his notebook pacing up and down the
street
Past the old-established Bull's Head, cooking old-established
meat.
In the old-established four-post bed he didn't get much sleep –
He was counting names of novels instead of old-established
sheep!

Pickwick Papers, American Notes
Don't forget your lecture tour from here to John-o-Groats.
Nicholas Nickleby, Dombey and Son,
Bleak House, Hard Times – a bundle of fun!
Is *Dorrit Little,*
Can *Oliver Twist?*
Oh, and little *David Copperfield,* I'll add him to the list!
Martin Chuzzlewit, a hero's rise to fame,
And *Our Mutual Friend* – that's a man without a name.
A Christmas Carol,
Household Words,
Romance in *Great Expectations* – that's strictly for the birds!
A Tale of Two Cities,
The Haunted Man,
The Mystery of Edwin Drood – solve it if you can.

He was the Dickens of a writer! What the Dickens did he do?
He brought the tourists to Beaumaris – and he brought me too!
Looking for a sign, for a plaque upon the wall,
'CHARLES DICKENS SLEPT HERE' – but it isn't here at all!

Henry's Wedding rap

Henry the Eighth
Was a suitor bold
With his bright red beard
And his Cloth of Gold.
He was famous for his singing
And his rhythm in the rap
Chatting up the chicks
Adding feathers to his cap.

Catherine of Aragon
Was first choice for Queen
A pretty Spanish redhead –
Success it should have been.
But she couldn't give him sons
For the Tudor line, no hope
So he filed for divorce
And he argued with the Pope.

His roving eye fell
On pretty Anne Boleyn
As fresh as a cherry
Ripe for marrying him.
But others liked the taste
And jealous Harry said,
'This fruit's gone rotten –
Quick, off with her head!'

Jane was his sweetheart
His very special date
She gave him a son
But her pain was great.
As she left this world
And closed life's door
She whispered, "You won't
See Jane Seymour no more!

Then he quickly fell in love
With a portrait fair
Of Anne of Cleaves
The Flanders mare.
But she wasn't like her picture
Just an ugly lass
So he unleashed her reins
And put her out to grass!

Catherine Howard seemed
A plump young wench
As she dallied with the old king
Behind the palace bench.
But she dillied with the courtiers
Who'd found a pretty catch.
Henry came and caught her –
Game, Set and Match!

Catherine Number three
Had been widowed twice
When Henry had a scheme
That she'd be quite nice –
Not the wicked creature
That stepmothers are
But for his three children
Both a Parr and Ma!

And so it happened
That the much-married king
Was survived by one –
When he'd had his fling
With a bevy of beauties
A perfect bunch of fives.
So Henry the Eighth –
He had six wives!

the ghost of
Twm Siôn Cati

Is there roguing in the tavern?
Are there hoof-beats down the lane?
Is that a rustle in the bushes?
Does Siôn Cati ride again?

With his smoking gun
And his sense of fun
Righting the wrongs
Where justice isn't done!

They say he had a rovin' eye, a passion for the girls,
He broke their hearts, he turned their heads, he stroked their
tumbling curls,
He married two, including Joe, and on their wedding day
Forged papers, proved where there's a will – there's certainly
a way!

They say he pinched a bucket from Llandovery's fine tin man
By complaining there were holes in every cauldron, pot and
pan,
'Put the pot upon your head,' Twm Cati boldly said,
'We'll have the rest while you try best to free your empty
head!'

They say he stole the finest horse a farmer ever bred,
And then he painted out its hide – 'twas grey not brindled red.
With cheek Twm took the painted beast to Brecon's mart again
And sold it back, his secret hid, until the evening's rain.

They say he tricked a highwayman he met upon the road;
With bags of shells he tempted him – the rogue thought they
                                                     were gold.
Over the hedge Twm threw his bags, the villain followed after,
But heard no chink of silver coins – just Twm Siôn's golden
                                                     laughter!

    Are there hoof-beats on the cobbles?
    Are there whispers down the line?
    Are there rustles in the bushes
    As in Mary Tudor's time?

        Is it Twm Siôn Cati?
        Welsh Dresser so natty
        Highwayman so chatty
        Drinking sweet café latte
        In the taverns of Tregaron and the Inns of Court,

        or is it Gentleman Thomas Jones?

a surfin 'set of seven'

Trek across the burning sand
Wet suit on and board in hand
Face the wave, get off the lip
Now's the time for a surfer's trip!

    ONE – fun
    on an off-shore breeze
    narrow your hips
    and bend your knees

    TWO – blue
    in the curl it's best
    at Langland Bay
    or Freshwater West

    THREE – D
    the ponshaped tails
    shaper's delight
    and knifey rails

    FOUR – score
    the highest break
    reef or point
    in Hell's Mouth wake

FIVE – live
with the new Surf tech,
transparent leash
and smooth dome deck

SIX – fix
for a surfboard bender,
catch the waves
on a summer ender

SEVEN – heaven
in a burning dream
through peaks and troughs
– Know what I mean?

Grab your boards and take a walk
To Llangennith beach, boys, hear this talk
Of *cutbacks, rockers, getting waves*
'Cos that's what every surfer craves.

Notes on the Poems

Jemima's Marching Song   p. 11
At the time of the Invasion of Fishguard in Pembrokeshire in 1797, the French soldiers were tricked into believing that a group of women, in traditional tall black hats and red shawls, and carrying pitchforks, were an army of British redcoats. The women were led by Jemima, a cobbler or shoemaker. She became known as the Fishguard saviour, the "General of the Red Army" who saved Britain from its last invasion by a foreign army!

Mari Lwyd Party   p. 13
The Mari Lwyd was a horse's skull, decorated with bells and ribbons, with glass eyes and felt ears. It was fixed to a long pole, and held by a man covered in a white sheet. At Christmas time, the Mari was carried from house to house by a group of men carrying lanterns. They knocked at the doors and sang rhymes asking to be let in. Once inside the houses, they were given beer to drink, while the Mari chased the girls, pretending to bite them, and the other men played games and performed tricks.

Lanzarote Funtime!   p. 16
On Thursdays many flights leave Cardiff International Airport, full of Welsh holiday makers on their way to Lanzarote, one of the Canary Islands. It's a volcanic beauty spot off the coast of North Africa. Cezar Manrique, an artist and sculptor, helped to create a National Park there, whose logo is a devil with a stick, Il Diablo.

Roundhead Routers' Rap   p. 19
Colby Moor, just three miles east of Haverfordwest, was the site of one of the most important battles of the English Civil War in Wales. It was a war between those who supported the King – the Cavaliers – and those who believed that the country should be run by Parliament, with no need for a Royal family – these were the Roundheads. On the evening

of August 1st, 1645, the Roundheads, led by Rowland Laugharne, met Major Generals Stradley and Egerton, and their Cavalier army. The battle was 'very fierce and doubtful near an hour' but the Royalist cavalry fled back to Haverfordwest castle, chased by the victorious Parliamentarians (Roundheads). Within a few weeks all the important Royalist castles, at Carew, Manorbier and Picton, as well as Haverfordwest, had surrendered to the Roundheads.

Sherwood Supper Rap   p. 21

Many of the old ballads of Robin Hood include verses about forest feasts and meals prepared under the greenwood trees. Robin and his band of Merry Men often entertained their captives (those rich men, like the Bishop of Hereford and the Butcher, whom the outlaws robbed to give money to the poor) to a delicious meal before 'relieving' them of cash, clothing and jewels.

In this poem several of Robin's band of outlaws – Little John, the seven foot giant; Allan-a-Dale, the ballad-singing minstrel; Friar Tuck, the hermit, and even Much, the miller's son – show off their cooking skills, like celebrity TV chefs, to Maid Marian. She was the legendary sweetheart of bold Robin, and the uncrowned queen of the forest kitchens.

The Ballad of Swansea Jack   p. 24

A 'Swansea Jack' is the nickname given to any man from Swansea. It reminds people of the time when the city was a famous seaport, and the great sailors wore 'jack-tarred' clothing to keep themselves dry.

The nickname is also a reminder of a famous black Labrador who lived with his owner William Thomas in the docklands area, Padley Yard, in the 1930s. Jack rescued a 12-year-old drowning boy from the dock-water in June 1931, and another person a few weeks later. He became famous in the local paper, and then the national newspapers, and became a tourist attraction, winning medals and a silver collar!

Sadly he ate some rat poison, and although the police offered a £25 reward for his 'killer', he was never found. After Jack died, aged seven years, a local stonemason carved a special gravestone for 'Swansea Jack', which you can still see on Swansea promenade.

Charles Dickens Didn't Sleep Here!   p. 33

Charles Dickens, the famous Victorian novelist, visited North Wales in the winter of 1859. He is known to have stayed at a hotel in Beaumaris called 'The Old Bull's Head' and complained in a magazine article that everything was *old established* – the bed, the chamberpot, the cutlery, even the food!

He came to Anglesey to interview the priest at Llanallgo, who had been helping English families to identify the victims of a terrible shipwreck. *The Royal Charter* had been returning from Melbourne in Australia with 493 passengers and 4 million pounds worth of gold, when she hit rocks and sank in Moelfre Bay on October 26th, 1859. It was a disaster in which 455 people were drowned.140 were buried in the churchyard, and Charles Dickens set up a fund to build a monument which is still there today.

The poem includes a list of many of Charles Dickens's novels. It's a good way to remember their titles!

Henry's Wedding Rap   p. 36

Most people remember what happened to Henry VIII's six wives by reciting the rhyme

> *Divorced, beheaded, died.*
> *Divorced, beheaded, survived.*

This rap poem uses some of the well-known, but not necessarily true, stories about the Tudor king's queens to help tell them apart!

The Ghost of Twm Siôn Cati   p. 40

Twm Siôn Cati was a highwayman from Tregaron – or was he?

Thomas Jones led a double life, at one time a "respectable gentlemen and landlord" well-known for his love of history and knowledge about genealogy (family trees). At other times he was thought to be a famous con-man and trickster, a sort of Welsh Robin Hood who robbed from the rich and gave to the poor. This poem tells of four of his most famous tricks – including double-tricking another highwayman.

AUTHOR PROFILE

Poetry can be serious – and it can be fun too!

I love reading serious poetry – I've always got at least one book of 'thinking' poetry on the carpet by my side of the bed, just within arm's reach – but I can't write serious poetry for toffee.

What I've found that I can write, and that children I meet seem to enjoy, is rhyming verse. It's amazing how easy it is to remember rhymes – and that's why I cram lots of details into poems like the Sherwood Supper Rap, the Charles Dickens piece, and the Roundhead Rap. The poem then becomes what's known as an *aide memoire* – a reminder of facts you want to remember, like the names of Henry's wives or Robin's band of merry men, or the castles that Cromwell's men captured in West Wales.

Other poems are just an excuse to play around with the language.

> *You need the rhythm, and you need the rhyme*
> *You need the ideas and you need the time*
> > *to play with sound*
> > *jiggle it around,*
> > *kick it to the ground*
> > *until you've found*
> *Just the right order, just the right pace*
> *And the number of words to fill your space!*

The idea for the Rugby Club Rumba was linked to one of those red 'infills' on BBC 1 Wales, which are used between programmes, where a couple dance the rumba in the rain, and the surfing song is the jargon that my son uses when he's talking 'surf' with his mates down on the Mumbles or at Freshwater West. Anything, anytime, any place is suited to a rap poem. I started the Lanzarote one as I was on the plane going out there, and polished it up on the return flight to Cardiff!

You ought to try writing one – and have fun!